Looking at Flight

Don Radford

Batsford Academic and Educational Ltd London

Typeset by Tek-Art Ltd, West Wickham, Kent
and printed in Great Britain by
R J Acford
Chichester, Sussex
for the publishers
Batsford Academic and Educational Ltd,
an imprint of B.T. Batsford Ltd,
4 Fitzhardinge Street
London W1H 0AH

ISBN 0 7134 4257 3

Contents

Acknowledgment

The Author and Publishers thank the following for their kind permission to reproduce copyright illustrations: George Allen & Unwin, for the photograph on page 39 (from Werner Nachtigall, *Insects in Flight*); Heather Angel, page 42; British Aerospace, page 19; British Airways, page 18; Cameron Balloons, page 9; The Daily Telegraph, page 16; Imperial War Museum, page 26; McDonnell Douglas Corporation, page 17; Ministry of Defence (RAE Farnborough) (Crown Copyright), pages 7, 15; NASA, page 27; Novus Publishing Ltd, page 41; RAF (Crown Copyright), pages 20, 25 (top); Ripmax Models, page 29; Royal Navy Public Relations, page 25 (bottom); R.S.P.B., pages 30 (left) (photograph by Richard T. Mills), 30 (right) (Derek Washington), 31 (William S. Paton); Science Museum, London, pages 4, 8 (left), 13, 14; Steve Thompson, page 23; John Topham Picture Library, pages 11, 34, 35, 37, 40, 43, 44; D. and K. Urry (Bruce Coleman), page 33. The pictures were researched by Sheila Gordon. The diagrams on pages 12, 17, 23, 24, 31, 32-3, 38, 39 and 46 were drawn by R. F. Brien.

Introduction

Have you been to a Pantomime? Even if you haven't, you probably know the stories on which they are based. We call them Fairy Stories, but really they were the stories grown-ups used to tell one another during the dark evenings of winter. Some of them are based on things that really did happen. Cinderella is supposed to be the story of King Cophetua and the Beggar-maid put into fancy dress and with modern additions to give extra interest.

One of the themes in folk tales, that turns up again and again, is that of men and beasts that can fly. Men have dreamed about flight and have told stories about it from the dawn of history. Ancient gods were often shown as winged beings, and even today people think of angels as having wings. Because man thought that the Gods could fly, he thought that flying was either magical or something that only gods could do. In either case, attempts to fly would be sure to bring down the wrath of the Gods and the luckless inventor would come to a sticky end. Bellerophon, on the winged horse Pegasus, tried to fly to the home of the Greek Gods, Mount Olympus, but Zeus struck him down. Daedalus and his son Icarus, escaping from Crete, made wings of feathers and fastened them to their shoulders with wax. Icarus daringly flew too near the Sun God. The wax melted and he fell to his death in the sea (*left*).

There have been many true stories of men trying to fly, using home-made wings. The Benedictine monk, Elmer of Malmesbury, Wiltshire, sometime around 1130 AD, flew for 200 yards from the tower of his abbey. Fortunately, he broke only his legs on landing. He was luckier than Abbasa Ben Firnasa, of Cordoba, Spain, who crashed to his death in 890; or the Italian, Giovanni Battista Danti, who died as the result of wing collapse in 1503. Right up to the present time, men have been killed, trying to imitate birds. It was only when would-be fliers put to one side their attempt to copy birds that man started his long journey to the Moon. There are two dates to remember, 21 November 1783 and 17 December 1903. On the first date, Pilatre de Rozier and the Marquis d'Arlandes made the first balloon ascent and were the first men to have truly flown. On the second date, Orville and Wilbur Wright made the first flights in a heavier-than-air aircraft which was fully controllable. There is one other date worth noting: 12 June 1979. Using all the resources of modern technology in the construction of his aircraft, Bryan Allen from California pedalled for nearly three hours and made the first man-powered flight from England to France. His aeroplane, Gossamer Albatross, had a wingspan of 96 feet and weighed only 55 pounds. How the shades of Daedalus and others must have rejoiced! But, before we get too swollen-headed, we must remember that the birds and the bees and the butterflies have been flying without too much trouble for many millions of years. Compared with the dragonfly, the first creature to fly, some 300 million years ago, man is only a Johnny-Come-Lately in the business of flying.

Kites: Gliders on a String

What a way to start a book on Flight, by talking about kites! However, it was by studying how kites were kept aloft by the wind, that men, during the nineteenth century, discovered the science of flying. More about that later.

The flying of kites is an ancient sport and is thought to have been invented in China some 3000 years ago. Even man-carrying kites were made, though the passengers were usually either drunk, condemned prisoners or daring hot-heads. There are many Chinese and Japanese stories telling of the use of man-carrying kites to escape from enemies or to carry out some daring deed or even a robbery — they too had their Superman heroes.

The Western World was well behind the East. Although crude kites were flown by the Greeks and Romans, it was not until the early 1400s that anything like our kites, with a head and a long tail, was made. Kite-flying became a very popular pastime, but it was ignored by the scientific world until the second half of the eighteenth century. Even then, it was only used as a tool, to lift things into the air. Benjamin Franklin carried out his experiment using a kite to show that lightning was due to electricity. He flew the kite into a thunder-cloud one day in 1749. The damp kite string acted as a conductor, and electricity travelled down the string and made a spark between a key dangling on the end and Franklin's knuckles. He was lucky not to be electrocuted.

It was Sir George Cayley who made a study of kites and kite-flying between 1799 and 1809, and made the first model glider. He used two kites mounted on a long stick, a large one for the main plane and a smaller one for the tail-plane. In the course of his experiments, he discovered many of the basic laws which govern the control of the flight of aeroplanes. He has been described by some historians as "the true inventor of the aeroplane."

Sir George Cayley made several full-size gliders that really did fly and did carry passengers. Unfortunately, much of his work was ignored by men seeking to fly.

During the nineteenth century many other experimenters used kites in their investigations into flight. George Pocock used them to propel a lightweight carriage, for four or five passengers, at speeds up to 22 mph.

In 1893 the Australian Lawrence Hargrave invented the box-kite. This was more stable and could lift greater weights than any previous kite. At the beginning of the twentieth century Sam Cody devised man-lifting kites and formed a detachment of the British Army. In November 1903 he successfully crossed the English Channel in a boat drawn by kites. The top photograph shows him (on the right) and an assistant holding one of his box-kites.

In 1899 the Wright brothers built a model kite-glider to test their ideas about controlling an aeroplane. Their model was a small glider held captive by a string; like a kite. It also had four control lines which were attached to the wings. The experiment was a great success and led to the construction of a man-carrying glider and ultimately to the first successful flight in 1903.

Cody in Britain and the Voisin brothers and Henri Farman in France used the box-kite shape in the design of some of the early aircraft. Cody was a practical genius who was unable to read or write. This led to his death, as he was unable to calculate the stresses in structures (the pushes and pulls in the different parts of his aeroplane) and only worked by experience and guess-work. One day his instinct failed him and he died in a crash.

In the fifteen years from 1893 until 1908 an enormous amount of research was carried out on kites, especially into constructing strong, lightweight structures. Many of the findings were of use in designing aeroplanes.

One last triumph of kites: in December 1901 Guglielmo Marconi made the first successful radio transmission across the Atlantic. His receiving aerial was raised by a kite to 400 feet. So it was, the kite had an important part to play in the development of the aeroplane and a small part in radio.

Balloons

Man began to conquer the air when he learnt to float in it. Although it is probable that the idea had come to a number of people in the past, it was the Montgolfier brothers in France who filled a paper bag with hot air and saw it rise in the air. Mind, it was rather a large bag, 57 feet high and 41 feet diameter. This huge bag was filled with hot air and smoke on 19 September 1783. Slowly it rose, carrying with it a sheep, a cock and a duck. After this successful ascent, Etienne Montgolfier constructed a man-carrying balloon (*right*). Pilatre de Rozier and the Marquis d'Arlandes made the first free flight on 21 November 1783. It was entirely successful and Mankind had made another giant stride forward.

At the same time as the Montgolfier brothers were carrying out their experiments, Professor Jacques Charles (of Charles' Law fame) worked

on the idea of filling a rubber-coated silk globe with hydrogen. This lighter-than-air gas had been discovered by the English nobleman and scientist Henry Cavendish in 1766. On 2 December 1783, Professor Charles and his co-pilot sailed aloft. On its second ascent, his balloon reached a height of 10,000 feet.

Soon, the sport of ballooning caught on and many flights were made. The English Channel proved no barrier to the intrepid aeronauts. The military recognized that a man carried aloft in a balloon could spy on the enemy. In a number of armies Balloon Corps were set up and were employed up to the end of the First World War. The first use of a balloon in warfare was during the battle of Fleurus, 26 June 1794 (*far left*). Captain Jean Coutelle of the French Army kept watch on the movements of the Austrian Army, who regarded the use of balloons as unsporting. The French won.

Balloons float in the air, as submarines or fishes float in water. The weight of the balloon acting downwards must be balanced by the lift acting upwards. This lift is equal to the weight of the air displaced by the balloon. If the lift is greater than the weight, then the balloon rises. If the lift is less than the weight, then the balloon sinks. As the density of the air becomes less as the balloon rises, the lift also becomes less. In the end, the lift equals the weight, so the balloon floats, neither rising nor sinking.

Balloons are blown by winds, without any control by the balloonists. Attempts were made to steer and propel the balloon with the aid of rudders and paddles. But, however hard man waggled rudders and heaved at paddles, nothing happened and the balloon drifted at the will of the wind. Rudders are useless unless the craft is moving relative to the fluid in which it floats. A balloon blown by the wind moves relative to the ground, but is stationary relative to the wind; so the rudder won't work.

Recently, ballooning using hot-air balloons has become a modern sport. Hot-air ballooning re-emerged because of two modern inventions: an envelope made of "rip-stop" nylon fabric that would not tear if punctured; and compact, lightweight propane cylinders and burners to

Cameron Balloons.

supply the heat to keep the air inside the balloon hot.

Today, non-flammable helium-filled balloons are used to obtain meteorological measurements. They take up small radio transmitters which relay back measurements of air pressure, temperature and humidity. Larger balloons of 10 million cubic feet and made of lightweight polythene film have ascended 30 miles high, taking-up with them scientific instruments and experiments.

Balloons may not be as glamorous as rockets, but they can be a powerful tool for scientific research.

Airships: Dinosaurs of the Air

By the middle of the nineteenth century it was painfully obvious that paddles and rudders were useless on a balloon. A method had to be devised to propel the balloon using some sort of engine, instead of leaving it to the mercy of the winds. At the time, the steam engine was the only engine available. It was heavy, as there were not only pistons and cylinders to carry, but the steam boiler and coal fuel as well. The problem was never solved until lightweight petrol and diesel engines were available, at the beginning of the twentieth century.

A Frenchman, Henri Giffard, in 1852 constructed an airship 143 feet long and powered it with a 3 HP steam engine weighing 350 lbs. Providing there was no wind blowing, the airship sped along at 5 mph, but was unable to turn or return to base. It was a gallant effort, but like so many inventions it was born before its time.

For the rest of the nineteenth century man learnt the hard way how to control airships, not just to go left or right, but how to go up and down as well. At the beginning of the twentieth century, with the development of lightweight engines, the airship became a practical proposition. In France and England airships were made like elongated balloons, with engines hung below them. But in Germany an entirely different airship was being developed. Count Ferdinand von Zeppelin built a lightweight, stiff, cylindrical framework of aluminium, streamlined at each end and covered with fabric. Inside this container were separate balloons filled with hydrogen. Beneath the envelope were hung gondolas, which housed the passengers, engines and crew. In 1910 the first commercial airline started carrying passengers in the *Graf Zeppelin*. During the First World War, Zeppelins became a menace to English cities, as they were able to carry a load of bombs at a height above the capabilities of the defending aircraft. As aeroplanes improved and developed methods of shooting them down, the Zeppelins grew bigger and faster. By 1918 they had a speed of 78 mph, a ceiling of 23,000 feet and a range of nearly 4000 miles.

All airships contained the seeds of their own destruction, the flammable gas hydrogen. Over and over again airships burst into flames. The *R101* crashed and burnt in 1930. The photograph shows the *Hindenburg,* 804 feet long and with over 7 million cubic feet of hydrogen, which caught fire at Lakehurst, New Jersey, U.S.A., as it was coming in to moor on 6 May 1937. Why it caught fire has not been satisfactorily explained. All sorts of theories have been put forward, but this disaster brought to an end the age of the giant airships. The dinosaurs of the air were extinct.

That might have been the end of the story, but for the non-flammable light gas helium. Filled with helium in place of hydrogen, airships would no longer be flying incendiary bombs. The U.S.A. had supplies of helium and during the Second World War ordered 200 airships, called Blimps, to escort slow merchant ship convoys. They were highly successful and no ship was ever lost when guarded by Blimps.

Today, the Goodyear Company build and operate Blimps for advertising missions. You may have seen their bulbous, streamlined shapes slowly gliding along in the quiet summer skies. A British company, Aerospace Developments, has built an experimental airship, *A.D. 500*, using modern plastics and high technology. It has been suggested that it could be used for transporting heavy loads in Britain or materials in Third World countries where communications are poor. Airships can carry heavy loads and do not require long runways for landing. They are quiet and cause a minimum of disturbance to the environment. Today they are safe. They could be used for Fishery Protection and as Flying Radar Stations. They have the advantage of being able to stay aloft for long periods. If they can live down their bad reputation, there may be a future for airships, although they are, and always will be, large and unwieldy.

Cayley, Lilienthal & the Wrights

The truly controllable aeroplane owes much to four men: from England, Sir George Cayley (1773-1857); from Germany, Otto Lilienthal (1848-96); and from the U.S.A., Wilbur Wright (1867-1912) and Orville Wright (1871-1948). Sir George Cayley has been titled the "Father of Aerial Navigation". He had an inquisitive and lively mind and investigated such different subjects as aeroplanes, land drainage, endless track tractors and artificial legs and arms.

The forces acting on a glider's wing during flight.

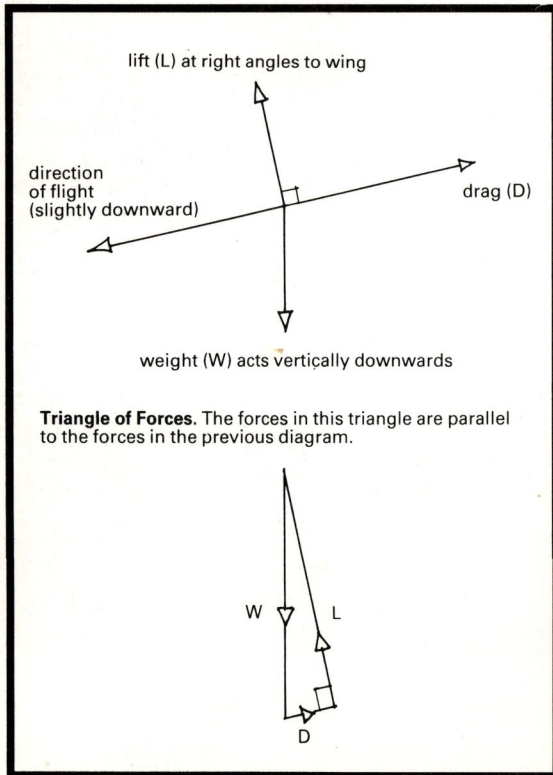

Triangle of Forces. The forces in this triangle are parallel to the forces in the previous diagram.

Cayley laid the foundations of a new science of aerodynamics. It was on this groundwork that later investigators were able to build.

Cayley separated the forces acting on a wing and recognized that man could never flap his wings and fly. Man simply isn't built like a bird and hasn't the muscular power to do it. Cayley built a number of gliders and made them so that they were stable and did not require someone to control them all the time. He built his gliders as you build paper aeroplanes; all the adjustments are made before launching, not during the flight. At least two people flew successfully in Cayley's gliders. In 1853 his footman flew from a hill across a valley. On landing, he quit his job.

The next of the quartet was Otto Lilienthal. From 1891 until his death in 1896 Lilienthal built and flew a number of gliders. In all, he made more than 2000 flights in what we would call today a hang-glider. His contribution was that he demonstrated how to control his gliders when in the air; he did not produce a stable aircraft but one which could be controlled by shifting his body weight, just as modern hang-glider pilots do.

In the closing years of the nineteenth century the Wright brothers, having succeeded in business making and selling bicycles, turned to a study of aeronautics. Right from the beginning, they built gliders that could be controlled in the air. To understand the control of aeroplanes, consider riding a bicycle. On reaching a corner, you turn the handlebars and lean inwards. To turn an aeroplane, the pilot turns the rudder and makes the plane bank, or lean inwards. Also, the pilot controls whether the plane climbs, dives or remains in level flight.

It took four years of experimenting, before the Wrights produced a motor-driven aircraft. (The

photograph shows the First Flight, 17 December 1903.) In that time they perfected the means of control and, as there were no suitable engines in existence, they designed and built their own engine. This weighed 180 lbs, produced 13 BHP *, and was based on motor car engines. They also had to design, test and make propellers to drive their aeroplane.

* BHP = Brake Horse Power; the maximum power produced by an engine before it is used to work machinery.

The Wright brothers brought together the skills and knowledge of many pioneers. They also added their own designs of plane control, propellers and engines. They overcame many difficulties by dogged determination, scientific logic and hard work.

At last, Man had truly flown and the stage was set for other men to follow the Wright brothers' example.

The String, Stick and Canvas Era

The world received the news of the Wright brothers with a deafening silence. Even their own country ignored them. European experimenters doubted the stories of Yankee flight, and so much of the Wrights' work was duplicated and all the old mistakes were repeated. By 1908 a number of Europeans had staggered into the air or had hopped short distances. Even the British Army had commissioned and received a plane from Sam Cody. The photograph above shows what a weird contraption it was. In August 1908 Wilbur Wright gave his first public flight in France. The Europeans were astounded. Leon Delagrange summed up their feelings: "Eh bien, nous sommes battus! Nous n'existons pas!" It was back to the drawing board with a grim determination to succeed. And succeed they did.

Whereas the Wrights almost vegetated, the Europeans pushed on vigorously. At Rheims, in the last week of August 1909, a great aviation "fly in" was organized. Much had been accomplished since Wright had had the Europeans gasping. On 25 July 1909 Bleriot had flown the English Channel; the world air speed record was raised to 47 mph; the record distance flown was 96 miles and the height reached was about 500 feet. Europe had become air-minded and vast strides were made in the new science of aerodynamics.

Two types of aeroplane were developed: the monoplane with one main wing, and the biplane with two main wings, one above the other. For a time, the biplane led, because the structure of two wings together was very much stronger than one wing on its own. It was not until new

materials came along in the 1930s that the monoplane really won the day. The problem to be solved was a simple one to state – how to construct a wing strong enough to support itself and the weight of the aircraft, without the "bird cage" arrangement of wires that were found between the wings of a biplane.

Surprisingly, the First World War did little to further the science of aerodynamics. Planes at the end of the war, like the SE5A (*above*), were only a little more advanced than the best of 1914. They were still made of wood, wire and canvas, just like the early planes. However, engines were more powerful, better-designed and more reliable than most of those available before the war. The planes were also more reliable, although still based on pre-war technology. The Avro 504 biplane was produced in 1913 and remained in service with the RAF until 1933. In the 1920s and early 1930s the biplane was the Queen of the Skies, ranging from small fighters to large airliners, and designs similar to the SE5A lasted until they were replaced by Hurricanes and Spitfires.

The years immediately after the First World War were marked by the adaptation of wartime aircraft for civilian use. Soon, designers turned to producing airliners and, with the formation

of airlines carrying passengers, a whole new crop of problems arose. The setting-up of aerodromes and the organization of flights were mingled with problems of navigation, servicing of aircraft and those of just handling the passengers. The U.S.A. developed a compact airways network covering the whole of the States, without the need for external routes. Great Britain, with its responsibilities at that time covering the whole of the globe, had to build up long-distance air routes. By 1929 Imperial Airways was operating a service to Karachi in what is now Pakistan.

Gradually, the age of the biplane was coming to an end. A new breed of airliners was beginning to appear in the sky. Firms like Fokker, Junkers, Douglas and Boeing designed and produced monoplanes; planes made of metal and not cluttered with the bracing wires and struts of the biplanes. Look at the photograph of the DC2 on page 17. This was one of the first airliners that looked anything like the planes in which you fly today. The stage was being set for a new era, but we must remember that, for a long time, the monoplane was the Cinderella of the story, overshadowed by the big sisters, Biplane and Triplane.

15

A New Shape: the Monoplane

△
A Spitfire MK IX of World War Two flying over a replica of a Sopwith triplane of World War One.

Really, the monoplane was not entirely new. It was a slow developer, mainly because of structural problems. In 1909 Bleriot had flown the Channel in a monoplane, but the wing was held in place by wires. The First World War broke out in 1914 and both sides deployed their aeroplanes as scouts. By the autumn of 1915 the Germans had established air superiority with their Fokker Eindecker*. As a plane, it was very much like the French Morane-Saulnier N, but it had an overwhelming advantage: a machine-gun firing through the arc of the propeller. There were several other monoplanes but none of them became stars. The biplanes and triplanes ruled the sky.

*German for monoplane.

In the air forces of the world, the biplane ruled the roost almost until the Second World War, because it was manoeuvrable. It could turn on the proverbial sixpence. But during the 1920s it became obvious that if you wanted speed, then the clean, streamlined monoplane was the answer. It was the Schneider Trophy races that hammered home the lesson. Great Britain won the races in 1927, 1929 and 1931, using a monoplane with floats. After that, all air speed records have been held by monoplanes. England and Germany soon became aware that the war of the future would be fought in the air using monoplanes. The Spitfire Hurricane and

Messerschmidt 109 were the fighter planes of the late 1930s and the Dorniers, Heinkels, Junkers, Boeings and Bristols were the bombers. These were the planes that in many cases could outrun the biplane fighter with ease.

The problems to be solved were enormous. Not only were there design problems, but there were operational problems as well – problems not even dreamed of with the slow and easy biplane droning its way across the skies. The monoplanes were faster and flew higher than their predecessors. At their operational heights, oils set solid, guns froze and the controls became less effective. The crew needed special clothes and oxygen to combat the cold and thin air at high altitudes. Not only that, but what is the use of a plane with a crew and a load of bombs if you cannot find your way in the dark? High-speed flying in the dark in wartime was something new. Technological progress in the Second World War was pushed to the limit and solving these problems helped civil aviation in peace-time. New materials were tested and used; new fuels and oils enabled engines to produce more power without blowing up; radar and radio were developed and became essential navigational aids.

During the 1930s the construction of the fuselage changed from one using wooden spars, fabric covering and wire bracing to one using thin metal sheeting stretched over stringers and fuselage formers. In the new design, the metal skin helped to carry some of the load. The old fabric covering added little to the strength of the structure. Metal skinning of the fuselage and wings enabled more streamlined shapes to be used.

One other important development was pursued by both German and British. This was the jet engine. More will be said about jet engines on pages 20-21, but it is sufficient to say that, with their introduction, air power made another giant step forward. Immediately, there were difficulties to overcome, because any step into the unknown has its dangers and problems and man was approaching an aeronautical barrier which was to change the whole of his ideas about flight.

Fuselage construction.

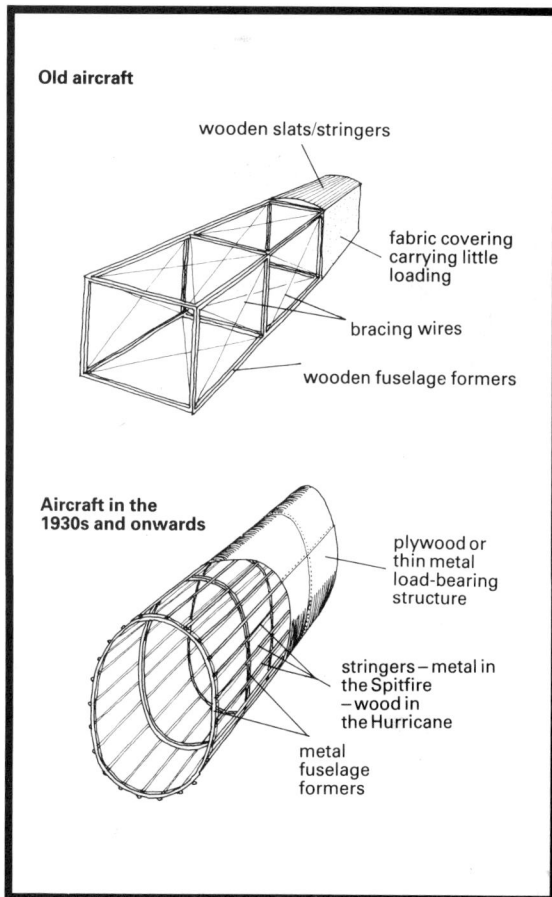

Old aircraft

wooden slats/stringers

fabric covering carrying little loading

bracing wires

wooden fuselage formers

Aircraft in the 1930s and onwards

plywood or thin metal load-bearing structure

stringers – metal in the Spitfire – wood in the Hurricane

metal fuselage formers

Modern Jet Aircraft

Some of the fighter planes in the Second World War were very fast and, if they dived under full power, soon pushed their speed to over 600 mph. Then strange things would happen; the plane would shake and buck like a wild horse and the controls would become heavy and less effective. Many a plane has lost its tail in a power dive. Sometimes it was because the pilot pulled out too steeply, but on many occasions the plane had run into what was called "compressibility problems". There was one Second World War fighter that was notorious for losing its tail. This was the Lockheed P38 Lightning.

The "compressibility problem" increased, the nearer the plane approached the speed of sound, because the air became more and more difficult to push to one side, and so became compressed. A similar thing happens when you push a broom through snow. The snow piles up until it becomes more and more difficult to push. Then it breaks away and large lumps of snow come back over the broom, and the broom becomes easier to push. Any object as it passes through the air, or if air is blown against it, causes the air to be compressed to some extent. The same laws of aerodynamics control the flight of a cricket ball as it swerves when bowled, or a garden fence during a gale, or Concorde in flight, or even a rifle bullet on its way to its target. For a time, it looked as though the speed of sound would be as fast as a plane would go. Yet bullets and shells exceeded the speed of sound. There was something wrong; so it was back to the drawing board and the laboratory. Finally, after much hard work, the problems were solved. The solution was to build planes with different shapes. For those whose top speed was less than 600 mph the old shape would do, after it was cleaned up. But, for those supersonic planes, the planes that would exceed the speed of sound, the shapes were very different. The wings would have to be swept back or in the form of a triangle (delta-shaped). Some planes, for example the Royal Air Force Tornado aircraft (see page 20), have wings that can be swept back in flight. For speeds below the speed of sound, called Mach 1, the wings are straight out. For supersonic speeds, the wings are swept

back.

Military planes weren't the only ones to change. Civil planes changed too. At first, airline companies used piston-engined, propeller-driven planes. But 1949 was the start of a new era for civil aviation, and for a time two British aeroplane companies led the world. De Havilland brought out the world's first jet-propelled civil airliner (*above*), and Vickers introduced the turbo-prop-engined Vickers Viscount. Unfortunately, being a pioneer often means paying a price for your daring. The aviation world was unaware of the dangers of metal fatigue, because metal had never been subjected to such pull, pushes and twists. It seems strange to talk about metals getting tired, but they do, and when this happens they break. It is not that the metal is being stressed beyond its maximum strength, but that it is constantly pushed, pulled and twisted beyond quite a moderate value. The problem was a new one. No one had ever met it before. In 1954 two Comets plummeted to disaster, one over the Mediterranean. When the wreckage was brought up from the sea bed and examined, it was found that metal fatigue around the windows had caused the fuselage to break up in mid-air. The aviation world learnt a bitter lesson, mainly at the expense of the British companies building and operating the Comet. In America Boeing used their "know-how" from producing military aircraft to build the first really successful civil jet aircraft, the Boeing 707. This plane has been the one against which all subsequent large jet-aircraft have been measured.

There is one plane however, which stands out on its own. It has no rivals; it is unique; this is Concorde. It is the only supersonic civil passenger airliner in service in the whole world. The difficulties building Concorde have been immense and technology has been pushed to the limit. While it may not be a financial success, it is a technological triumph and one of which France and the United Kingdom can be very proud.

Jet Engines

The Second World War showed that the piston engine and the propeller were reaching the end of the road. They had reached their practical limits. Propellers could not be turned any faster without running into problems. Engines and propellers could not be made bigger without becoming too large for the aircraft. The answer seemed to be a new form of propulsion – some form that was more compact and would deliver more power than the piston engine.

A similar problem had occurred with the steam engine at the end of the nineteenth century. As a result, the steam turbine had been developed to replace the steam piston engine. An attempt was made in the 1930s by Frank Whittle to produce an internal combustion gas turbine. The difficulties to overcome were enormous: the blades of the turbine work in burning gases and become red hot; they revolve not at a leisurely 2000 – 3000 rpm, but at tens of thousands of rpm; the bearings have to stand up to very high temperatures. Success in the jet engine had to wait for new metal alloys to be invented. During the Second World War both Britain and Germany developed the jet engine and used it to produce an enormous backward gale. This backward gush of gases thrust the plane forward, just as a downward jet of gases from a rocket sends it into the sky.

In a jet engine there are five different sections. Look at the diagram of a turbo-jet engine:

1. The air enters the engine through the *air intake*.
2. It is then *compressed* by the compressor.
3. Fuel is sprayed into the *combustion chamber,* where it burns.
4. As the hot gases leave the combustion chamber they turn a *turbine* . . . which supplies

RAF Tornado. Like the FIII, its wings can be swept back in supersonic flight.
▽

the energy to turn the compressor.

5. The exhaust gases then leave the jet engine and provide the *thrust* to move the aircraft.

By increasing the size of the turbine, more energy can be supplied to the compressor drive shaft than is needed to compress the gases. The excess energy can be used to drive a propeller in an aeroplane or a ship. See diagram B. Such an engine is called a turbo-prop engine if it is in an aeroplane, or a gas turbine if it is used to drive a ship's propeller or an electrical generator in an electricity power station.

There is an engine that is halfway between a turbo-jet and a turbo-prop engine (diagram C). The turbine powers a large fan that moves a great mass of air outside the turbo-jet. This large amount of air helps to quieten the jet noise and it makes the jet engine more efficient at the lower speeds of civilian aircraft.

If we look at the power of a jet engine compared with the last generation of piston engines, we can see what an enormous step has taken place. A 1945 Rolls-Royce Griffin engine could produce more than 2500 HP. The Rolls-Royce Olympus jet engines, used in Concorde, are rated at 38,050 lb. thrust; the maximum speed of Concorde is 1354 mph; there are four engines; at full speed and maximum thrust, the power of the four engines amounts to a total of 549,601 HP! There is the secret of the jet engine – it has power to spare, but it has a terrible thirst. If you want to go fast, you will have a heavy fuel bill.

A. Turbo-jet engine.

B. Turbo-prop engine.

C. Turbo-fan engine.

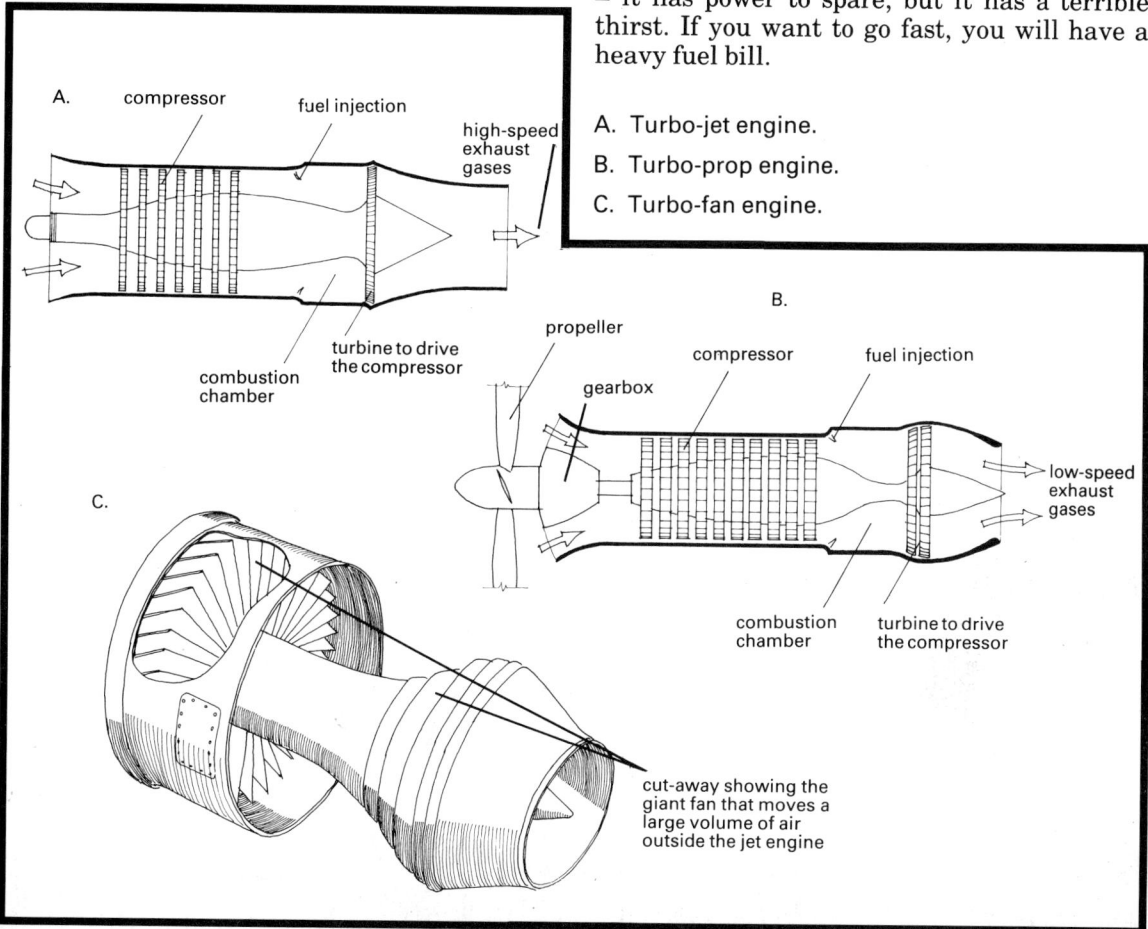

A. compressor   fuel injection   high-speed exhaust gases

combustion chamber   turbine to drive the compressor

B. propeller   gearbox   compressor   fuel injection   low-speed exhaust gases

combustion chamber   turbine to drive the compressor

C. cut-away showing the giant fan that moves a large volume of air outside the jet engine

Gliders and Man-Powered Flight

For thousands of years Man tried to imitate birds. If he was lucky, he escaped with a broken leg or arm; if not, then he paid for his mistakes with his life. It was not until the nineteenth century that Man realized that he hadn't muscles in the right places for him to compete with birds. The more scientifically minded turned to gliders. Starting with Sir George Cayley and ending with the Wright brothers, there is a list of men who furthered the progress of the aeroplane through their efforts at gliding. Otto Lilienthal was the most successful of nineteenth-century experimenters. He built and flew what we would call today a hang-glider and by the time of his death by accident in 1896 he had made nearly 2000 flights. Percy Pilcher in England, and Octave Chanute and the Wright brothers in the U.S.A. carried on with work on gliding. Even after the invention of the motorized aircraft men still experimented with gliders.

As a sport, gliding started after the First World War, at Wasserkuppe, Germany, 1920. Since then it has become a world-wide sport and modern gliders are designed with the care and skill of a fighter plane. They are built of modern materials and are not a bit like the bamboo, string and fabric machines of the pioneers.

How does a glider work? What keeps it up? Look at the diagram on page 12. A glider has acting on it three forces: the LIFT of the wings, the WEIGHT of the glider and pilot, and the DRAG as it goes through the air. These three forces can be represented by a triangle of forces, something that Sir George Cayley knew way back in the eighteenth century. Notice that the direction of flight is always downwards with respect to the air, so unless the air is moving upwards faster than the glider is falling downwards, the glider will come to earth. If the air is moving upwards fast enough, the glider will stay up.

The next question is, "Where do you find air moving upwards?" There are four cases of rising air generating lift:
1. Wind blowing against a slope.
2. Doughnuts of hot air rising – these are known as thermals.
3. Rising air under clouds – the winds under and within a thunder cloud are very violent and are dangerous even to powered aircraft.
4. To the lee side of mountains where wind forms "standing waves". The bottom diagram shows where lift can be found.

Some birds use lift to help them fly. Look inland for gulls lazily soaring round and round. Most likely they have found a rising thermal. Look out for them at the seaside, riding the rising air as the wind blows against a cliff or sea wall.

From bird flight let us turn once again to man flight, that is a man propelling and keeping himself aloft by the power of his muscles alone. Unfortunately, we aren't very good producers of energy. The author has carried out a large number of tests on adults and has found that most can only produce 0.1 HP steady power, a few 0.2 HP and even fewer 0.4 HP. It is said that a champion cyclist can put out about 1.3 HP for a few seconds. So, as the power is low, any man-powered aeroplane must be as light and as efficient as possible. It is only recently that lightweight and strong enough materials have been available. Man-powered flight owes more to technology and the skill of the designer than to the power output of Man. With hang-gliders, man has only to hang on. He keeps aloft by making use of rising air and controls the glider by moving his body from side to side and to and fro.

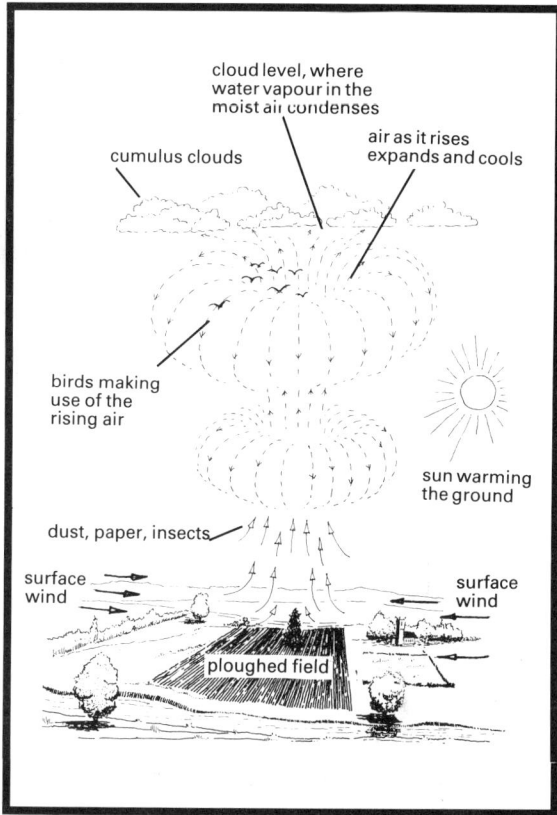

Thermals – doughnuts of rising air.

Hang-gliders are fun. How the shades of Lilienthal, Pilcher and Chanute must rejoice at seeing something very much like their own creations! At least they would be familiar with the controls, if not with the materials from which the gliders are built. Man has achieved flight using his own muscles, but only with the aid of very high technology.

Slope lift and standing waves.

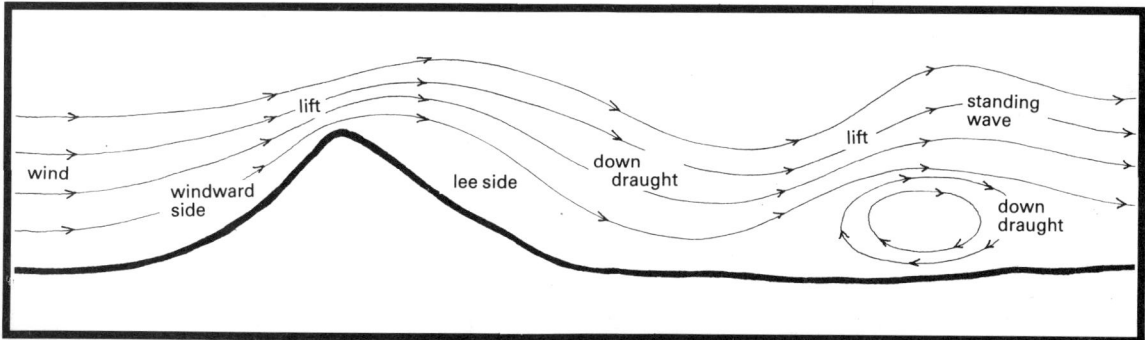

Helicopters and Autogiros

Scarcely a week goes by but we see on the TV screen pictures of helicopters at work. We see them taking men to drilling rigs in the North Sea; carrying out Sea Air Rescue missions; taking people from one place to another; landing in the midst of cities or jungles; taking urgent stores and medical supplies to disaster-stricken areas; as military troop and weapon carriers. (A double rotor helicopter like the Chinook in the top photograph can carry a payload of nearly 10 tons for a distance of 250 miles.) The helicopter is without equal where some form of transport is needed to deliver something in a space not big enough for the landing of a fixed-wing aeroplane.

That is the clue to its usefulness. The normal aeroplane, that is, the one with fixed wings, flies because, as it flies, wind over the wings produces lift; the faster the plane goes the greater is the lift. If the plane slows down, the wind is less and so is the lift. But the wings of the helicopter are the rotating blades on top of the fuselage driven by a motor. The helicopter does not have to move forward to produce lift, only make the rotor blades rotate. There are several snags that had to be overcome.

Snag No. 1   Consider the helicopter in sketch A. The rotor blade in position A is moving at 150 mph and, as the helicopter is moving forwards at 100 mph, the air is moving over the blade at (100 + 150) mph. Now look at the blade in position B. It is moving backwards at 150 mph and forwards at 100 mph, so the air is moving over it at (150 − 100) mph. The lift of a wing or rotor blade depends on the speed of the

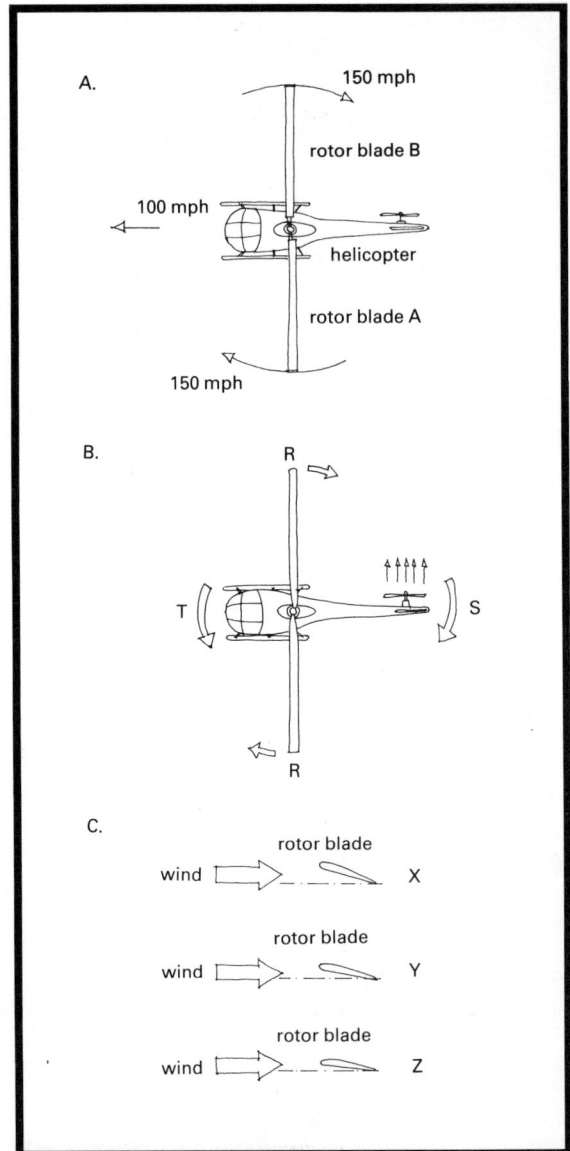

A.

B.

C.

A. Snag No. 1.

B. Snag No. 2.

C. Changing the angle of the rotor blades.

Autogiros

An autogiro looks something like a helicopter. It has rotating wings, but these are not permanently coupled to an engine. The forward motion of the autogiro causes the rotor blades to turn. An autogiro can take off and land in a fraction of the space a normal plane takes to do so; it is mechanically simpler than a helicopter, so there is less to go wrong; also it is cheaper to make and run than a helicopter. So far, no one has tried to make a large autogiro. It has not advanced much beyond a two-seater model, being eclipsed by the larger helicopters. A very manoeuvrable autogiro (*below*), designed and constructed by Wing Commander Wallis, has been used in James Bond films.

air over it. Air at 250 mph will provide more lift than air at 50 mph. So the lift on one side of the helicopter is greater than the lift on the other side.

Fortunately, there is one way to even the lifts so that they are the same. Lift also depends on the angle at which a wing or a rotor blade meets the air. Look at the wings X, Y and Z (sketch C). They meet the air at decreasing angles. Which provides the most lift? It is X. So the angle of the blades must be automatically changed as they go round. In position A the rotor blade must be at less of an angle than in position B. By altering the angle of the blade as the rotor goes round, the lift is kept constant.

Snag No. 2 (sketch B) If the rotor blades move round (R), then the body of the helicopter tends to move in the opposite direction (T). This can be opposed by having a propeller (P) at the end of the body. The propeller tends to push the body round (S), in an opposite direction to T. So T and S cancel each other out.

25

Rocket and Space Craft

Look up into the sky on 5 November and what do you see climbing on a jet of flame? Rockets have been known ever since the invention of gunpowder and once upon a time they contained slow-burning gunpowder to power them on their way. Nowadays the name rocket is given to all sorts of devices, from those used as fireworks to the mighty Saturn rockets used to launch the Apollo missions to the Moon. They may differ in size and burn different fuels, but they all have one thing in common. They all produce large amounts of very hot gases that are squirted out at a high velocity through a nozzle. It is these escaping gases that make a rocket go.

If you take a balloon and blow it up, then release it without tying the neck, it will whizz around until it is flat. The air escaping backwards, pushes the balloon forwards. This is an example of Newton's third law of motion: "To every action there is an equal and opposite reaction." A rocket works because large amounts of very hot gases are produced by the burning of fuel. This fuel may be solid or liquid and during the burning it is oxidized to form a gas. When we burn fuels in our motor cars, the petrol is oxidized by the oxygen in the air. All rockets carry their own oxidizing materials, so that they do not have to rely on the air to supply oxygen.

The amount of "thrust" the gases give the rocket depends on a number of things, one being the velocity of the exhaust gases. This has to be very fast indeed. In the German Second World War rocket V2 (*below*), the gas velocity was 6,700 feet per second (approx. 2000 m sec^{-1} or

4500 mph). Now to change the direction of an aeroplane there are elevators, ailerons and rudders. These act on the air and make the aeroplane climb or dive, bank and change direction. But, if a rocket goes high enough, there is little or no air and so elevators, ailerons and rudders are useless. Space rockets are steered by small rockets giving them a nudge in the right direction or by moving the jet of gas to point in another direction.

Once you have lit the touch paper of your 5 November rocket you have no further control of how long the rocket fuel will burn. This is a disadvantage of all solid-fuelled rockets. So solid-fuel rockets are mostly used for lift-off, while liquid-fuel rockets are used for steering.

Vast strides have been made in rocket technology. In 1971 the 363-feet-high Saturn V rocket was used to lift Apollo 15 and its crew to the Moon. (*above left*). When they returned, the Saturn rocket was scrap lying at the bottom of the Atlantic Ocean; some of their vehicle was left in space, and the splash-down module in which they returned was junk.

Today, the space-shuttle (*above*) is re-usable and its rocket tubes, which are discarded in flight, are recovered, refilled and re-used.

Models

On pages 12-13 you read of the contributions the Wright brothers made to the evolution of the aeroplane. They emphasized that the pilot must be able to control the plane and in order to find out about controls, they built models first, then man-carrying gliders, and finally an engine-powered aircraft. The models came first.

So we can say that there are two types of models: those we play with and those which are used for some useful purpose. The Wright brothers built a wind tunnel in which to test their ideas on models. It was cheaper and far less hazardous to work with models than full-sized aircraft.

The Wrights were not the first to use model aeroplanes for testing a theory. Sir George Cayley in the eighteenth century used them. So did W.S. Henson, John Stringfellow, Felix du Temple and others in the nineteenth century. Today, models are used not only in the aeronautical industry but in ship building and civil engineering. Before the Severn and Humber bridges were built, models of them were built and tested in wind tunnels, to see the effects of high winds. Such testing of models might have prevented the Tacoma bridge disaster in the U.S.A. forty years ago. During a gale the bridge swayed and twisted so much that it tore itself to pieces.

Radio-controlled model aircraft have been put to serious use, for forest fire spotting in Canada; taking aerial photographs for archaeologists; and in target practice for the military. It is very expensive building full-size antique aircraft for use in films, so nowadays the dogfights between Camel and Fokker are filmed using radio-controlled scale models.

The first of the illustrations shows a model of a Morane-Saulnier P monoplane (1916-17), which has been used to show how the wings and

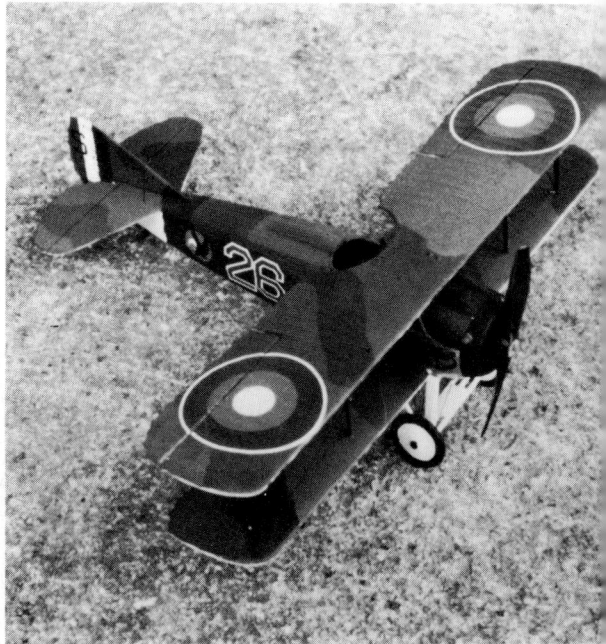

fuselage were constructed. The second illustration is of a model Spad XIII (1917-18). It is painted in camouflage colours, greens on the top surfaces and yellowish cream for under-surfaces. This has been used in biology classes showing how man has copied nature when hiding from enemies. The other two photographs show close-ups of models. It is very difficult to see whether the subjects are models or full-sized aircraft.

Radio-controlled aeroplanes are great fun to fly. They can be made to perform acrobatics even more complicated than the real thing. The same laws of aerodynamics control their flight, as control any full-sized subsonic plane. They are built to withstand, in proportion to their size, greater strains and stresses than a full-sized fighter plane. As a sport, model aircraft flying is worldwide, and international competitions are as keenly contested as any world football match.

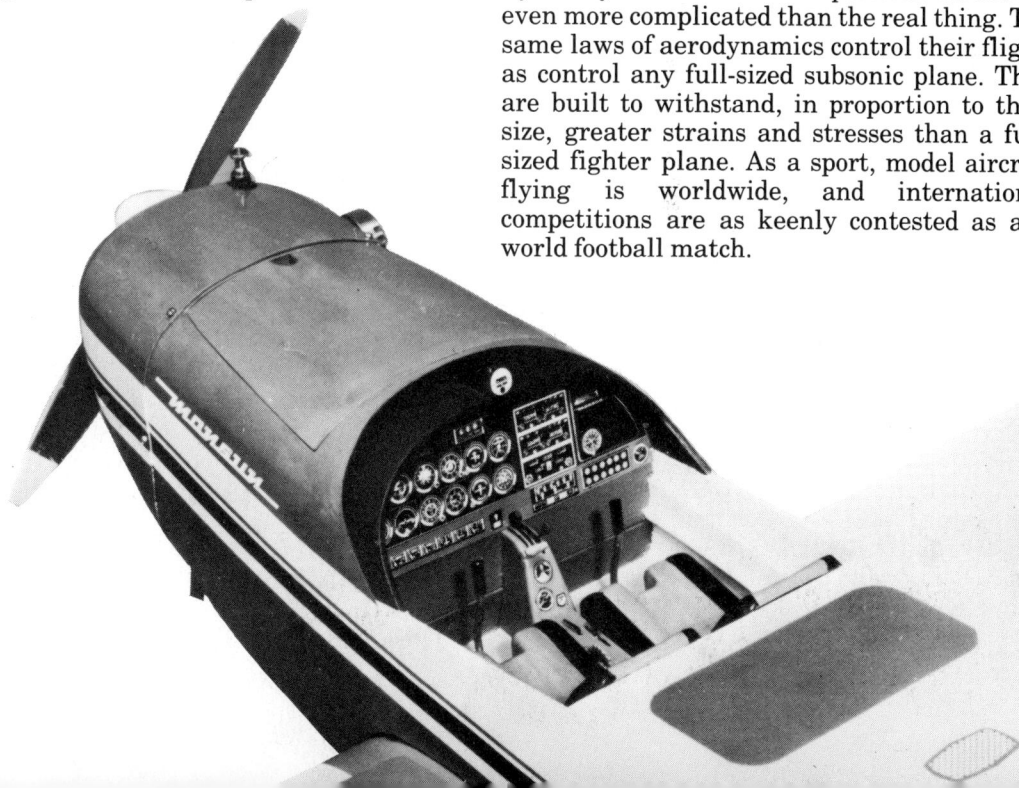

Birds: Gliders and Hoverers

Gulls, Albatrosses, Vultures, Buzzards

These birds are the gliders of the bird world. The albatross with its 11½-feet wingspan is the largest sea bird. Its home is the oceans of the southern hemisphere. In these regions of the world the winds blow constantly and were known to the sailing ship seamen as the "Roaring Forties".

The gulls and albatrosses have long, narrow wings like the wings of a man-made glider. These are more efficient than the broad wings of the eagles, vultures and buzzards. The sea birds need great efficiency as they roam the oceans out of sight of land. That is, they must be able to fly as far as possible for a given amount of food.

Albatrosses are able to fly long distances because they make use of rising air which is formed when the wind strikes the side of waves.

Over land, the bird gliders make use of thermals and slope lift (see the section on Gliders, pages 22-23). They need to be manoeuvrable so that they can seek out and stay in the doughnut (thermal) of rising air. Short wings can be turned more easily than long wings, a fact that was made use of in the First World War when fighter planes like the Sopwith and Fokker triplanes were amongst the most manoeuvrable planes ever built. The eagles, hawks and harriers are birds of prey and need to be manoeuvrable to catch their dinners. Their wings are short, broad and rounded.

Kestrels, Humming Birds

These are nature's helicopters. They hover and appear to be stationary in the sky, with only their wings fluttering, when searching for food. The hovering kestrel (*below*) is a quite common sight, even in our cities. Kestrels belong to a group of birds called Falcons. The peregrine falcon has been timed in a dive, by an aeroplane, to be doing more than 175 mph. The swept-back wings of all falcons are admirably suited for high-speed flight. They have a wingspan of between 15 and 19 inches. Contrast that with the albatross's 11½-feet wingspan.

The humming bird is another bird in a hurry. Its wing form is very much like that of the falcon, but it has a wingspan of only about 4 inches. When it is hovering, its wings beat at a rate of from 50 to 80 times a *second*.

Swifts, Swallows and House Martins (*above*)
These are quite small birds, but can they fly!
They feed on the wing, catching flying insects.
The swift is a remarkable aerial acrobat and he
often seems to do it for fun. One summer
evening the author watched a group of swifts
having fun. There was an old hut with a hole in
the door about 4 inches wide and a foot long (A).
In the side of the hut was a window with a
broken pane of glass (B). The hut was about 5
feet wide and 10 feet long, the door being on the
shorter side and the window on the long side.
The swifts were playing follow my leader. One
would dive on the hut, shoot through the hole in
the door and then a fraction of a second later,
come out of the broken window. Both holes
would have required the birds to fold their
wings for them to get through. How they made
the right-angled turn inside the hut, I have no
idea, but their skill left me gasping.

Birds: Ordinary Flappers

Most of the birds not mentioned in the last section can be grouped together, because there is nothing extraordinary about their flight. They just flap their wings and fly, don't they? But, if they only move their wings up and down, then the down-stroke is cancelled out by the up-stroke, so how do they fly? For a long time this remained a mystery. It wasn't until high-speed photography was available that the mystery was solved. Birds do not just flap their wings up and down – they twist them as well. A pigeon moves its wings downwards and partly forwards on the way down; then upwards and completely forwards on the way up. At this point the tips of its wings are forward of its head. Then comes a partly down-and-up stroke to complete a cycle of wing movements. The wing tip traces out a figure of eight pattern. The feathers in the wing tips are most important. They do much of the work by turning and screwing their way into the air.

A bird's wing consists of three working parts. The inner part, like an aeroplane's wing, provides lift when the bird moves through the air. The outer portion of the wing, corresponding to our hand, carries out most of the flapping and provides some of the power to drive the bird forwards. (The outer and inner parts of the wing can be moved separately.) To the outer portions are attached the big wing

The movement of a pigeon's wings during flight.

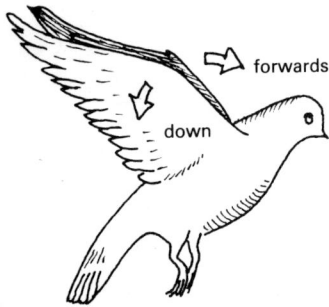

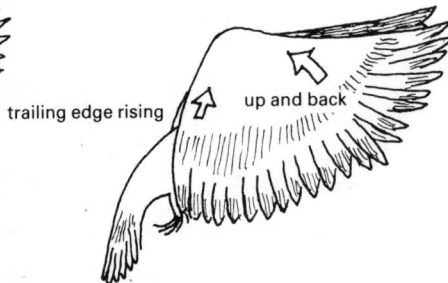

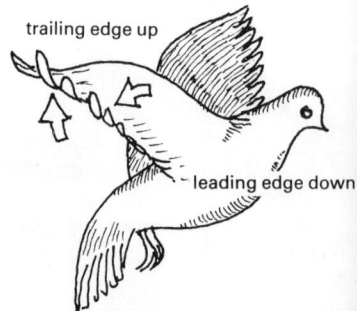

forwards

down

forward

fully down

up

trailing edge rising

up and back

trailing edge up

leading edge down

feathers which, as the wings beat, screw their way into the air. A bird's wing gives both lift and thrust.

The wings of a bird are worked by the muscles of its breast. This is the part of the chicken we enjoy so much when we eat roast chicken. All that white meat is muscle, and all that muscle is needed to flap the wings. Compare a chicken's muscles for flight, with our muscles moving our arms. A bird's wings can be compared with our arms and hands; there are similar bones in each; but weight for weight the bird has much more muscle than we have. No wonder man has never managed to use his arms as wings – not even Superman has enough muscles!

A bird's wings serve another useful purpose. When a bird or an aeroplane comes in to land, both have to slow down. The aeroplane does it by using flaps which increase the drag. A bird does it by rotating its wings until they present the greatest area to the direction of flight. Watch birds coming into land and how they almost stop in mid-air and then drop the last few inches.

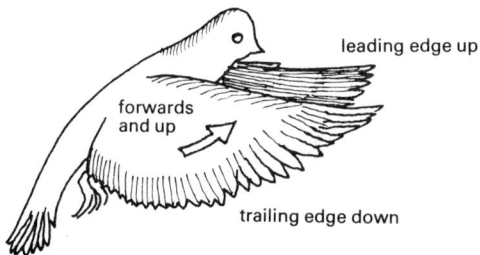

leading edge up

forwards and up

trailing edge down

fully up

Bats: Flying Radar Stations

Bats are regarded as mysterious creatures of the dark, and no good horror film is without its quota of bloodsucking vampires! It is a pity that all bats are regarded with suspicion just because some bats of South America feed on blood. Most bats live on insects. They catch them in the dark. The bats we are likely to see in Britain on a summer's evening are harmless creatures. When it has its wings folded the bat is about the size of a mouse. In fact, the Germans call it *Fledermaus* (fluttermouse) and the French name it *chauve-souris* (bald mouse).

Bats are mammals. They do not have fur or feathers. Their wings are made of skin stretched over bones and correspond to our arms and hands. They are nocturnal, that is, they come out to feed at night. Bats in Britain hibernate during the winter. This enables them to survive the wintertime when insects are scarce. During hibernation their blood temperature drops almost to the temperature of their roost. Their heart beats every couple of seconds, a huge drop from 1000 beats per minute during flight.

All things that fly, birds, insects, bats, or aeroplanes, must have wings (aerofoil surfaces) and a means of propelling them through the air. In aeroplanes, the means of propulsion is separated from the aerofoil. With animals and insects, the wings provide propulsion and the aerofoil surface. The nearest man-made equivalent is the helicopter, in which the main rotor blades provide both lift and propulsion.

A bird's wing is covered with feathers; a butterfly wing has a scaly covering; and a bat's wing is skin-covered. All these wings have a convex-shaped upper surface. The aerofoil surface of a bat's wing is formed by skin stretched over long thin fingers and is joined to the bat's legs and body. The bats' wing bones bear a resemblance to the bones of our hands, and upper and lower arms. Where we have a particular bone, so have the bats, but the relative sizes are different. Bats have fingers that may be longer than the rest of their arms.

When bats flap their wings, the paths they describe are similar to the paths of bird wings during flight. On the downward stroke the fully outstretched wings move forwards as well as downwards, until the tips are well ahead of the bats' heads. This provides lift and propulsion. On the upward stroke the wings are partially closed and, as well as moving up, they also move forward. The backward stroke provides most of the thrust.

In birds it is the large muscles in the breast that operate their wings. Bats use more muscles. The differences in the sources of power between birds and bats may be due to their different evolutionary ancestors. Birds are most likely descended from reptiles, whereas

mammals, of which bats are but one species, are much more ancient. It is likely that the ancestors of mammals broke away from reptiles many millions of years before the birds developed. Certainly in the Triassic period, 225-190 million years ago, well before the age of the dinosaurs, there were mammal-like reptiles and it is from these that we, and other mammals, developed.

Bats have a lot going for them. One in five mammals is a bat. They are the only mammals that really fly. Others can glide but no others can fly. They are able to catch their prey in the dark with amazing skill. But they are still victims of ignorance and prejudice.

Moths and Butterflies Flutter By

What is the difference between Moths and Butterflies? Like many simple questions, it is a difficult one to answer. There is no one difference between all butterflies and all moths. However, the following will give a rough but not always accurate guide:

Butterflies fly by day.
Butterflies rest with wings vertical.
*All Butterflies have antennae with knobs on the end.

Moths fly by night.
Moths rest with wings flat.
Moths' antennae have no knobs and are usually thin or feathery.

But there are exceptions to all these statements, except the one marked with a *. Don't worry about the distinction between moths and butterflies. It is an artificial one.

Butterflies and moths belong to a group of insects called the Lepidoptera, which means "scale wings" (Greek: *lepis pteron*). Their wings are wonderfully made. First of all, they are curved, like the top surface of an aeroplane wing; this shape is a much more efficient flying shape than a flat sheet. Then the surface is covered with tiny scales that overlap like the tiles on a roof. These scales give the patterns and colours of moths and butterflies. The colours are formed in the same way as a drop of motor car engine oil produces colours on a wet road. The process is called the Interference of Light.

Under the wing scales there are two membranes, each less than one ten-thousandth of a millimetre thick and kept apart by veins. When a butterfly first comes out of its chrysalis, its wings are crumpled and limp. A special liquid is pumped into the veins and spaces between the two membranes, to blow up the wings in the same way as you can blow up a balloon. This liquid hardens and, after about an hour, sets solid. The veins become solid rods that stiffen the wings rather like the ribs of an umbrella or the spars of an aeroplane wing. It is very important that the wing-hardening process is uninterrupted, because it cannot be stopped or reversed. A crumpled wing that hardened as a crumpled wing stays crumpled and cannot be used for flight.

Moths and butterflies each have two pairs of wings. The front and back wings may be coupled together in a manner rather like the fastenings of two strips of velcro. They can uncouple their wings when resting.

As well as flying by flapping their wings, butterflies and moths can also glide. With their small weight and relatively large wing area, their speed of gliding is quite low. This means that if they were gliding into a gentle breeze, their speed of gliding might be the same as the speed of the wind. They would hover. If the wind speed was greater than their gliding speed, they would fly backwards! So, gliding is strictly for calm summer evenings, or during migration, when winds help butterflies and birds to cover long distances. Being light, they are also easily carried up in thermals of rising air.

All engines need energy. A butterfly is a living flying engine and has to be powered with fuel. Most butterflies and moths rely on nectar produced by flowers. This material is a solution of sugars in water. Some migrating butterflies, in order to keep their engines running and to cut down unnecessary weight, need concentrated forms of fuel. They sip nectar and then convert the sugars into fat which they store. Fat is a very efficient fuel. To cover the same distance, an insect using fat as a fuel carries only one-eighth of the fuel it would have to carry if it used sugar.

To get energy from a fuel, the fuel must be oxidized. Land and air animals use oxygen in the air to oxidize fats and sugars. We breathe air into our lungs, extract some of the oxygen from it and breathe out waste air and carbon dioxide, one of the products of oxidation. Butterflies and other insects do not have lungs. Air enters their bodies by small openings called spiracles. These join large distributing trachea, which supply muscles directly with oxygen. In our bodies oxygen is transported from the lungs to the muscles by the haemoglobin in the blood. Insects move the oxygen around by squeezing and dilating the trachea system. On a small scale, the insect method of supplying muscles with oxygen is very efficient, far more efficient than our own method. Humans can achieve a five-fold increase in energy output from steady work to flat out (the same is approximately true for car engines), but insects can multiply their energy output from 14 to 100 times. This staggering increase in energy explains why some insects are good fliers and generally are a very efficient class of animal life. They comprise the largest class in the animal kingdom.

Other Flying Insects

In the last section, the flight of butterflies and moths was mentioned. We know a lot about insect flight through the researches of biologists like Professor Werner Nachtigall. His book *Insects in Flight* is a fascinating account of the structure of insects and how they fly.

Like birds, insects do not just flap their wings up and down. They twist their wings as they flap, so that sometimes the wings provide lift and sometimes they provide thrust. We will deal here with two aspects of insect flight: how they move their wings; and the engine or mechanism that drives their wings.

First of all then, the path of the wing during flight: many insects flap their wings so fast that they look blurred. The secrets of flight have been revealed by using high-speed cameras that take a picture in a millionth of a second (10^{-6} sec). In such pictures, the wings – even of a busy bee – appear to be still. By taking hundreds of pictures, the paths of the wings can be traced. Look at the diagram below. It shows what you would see if you had high-speed eyes and if you looked at a fly as it flew past you. The fly does

The path of a fly's wing during flight. —◦ represents the wing. ◦ is the leading edge.

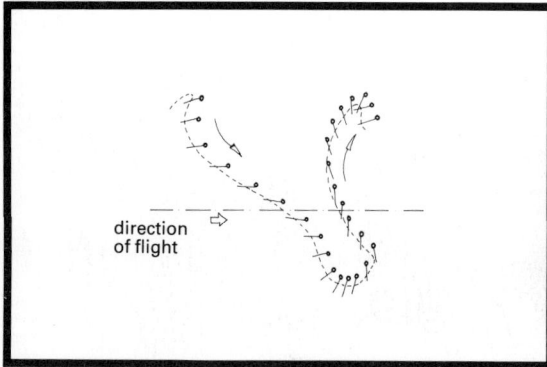

Dragonfly power.

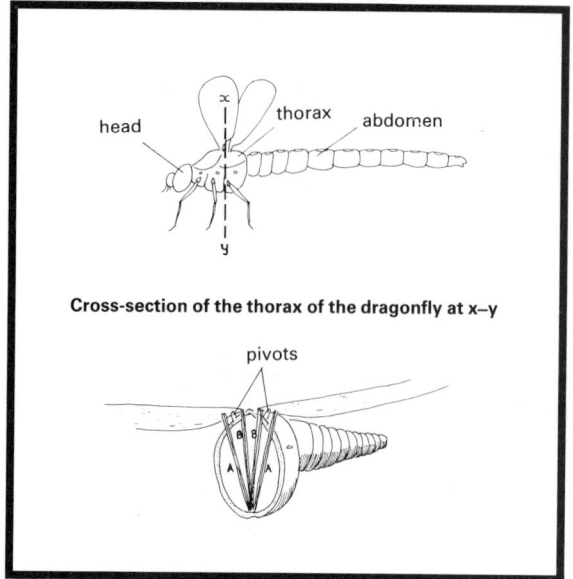

Cross-section of the thorax of the dragonfly at x–y

flap its wings up and down, but, most important of all, it twists its wings. Twists like this occur in the flight of birds, bats, butterflies, moths and insects in general. This is the secret of animal flight and is one of the reasons why men, stiffly flapping their arms up and down, could never hope to fly. Most of the flying animals can glide by holding their wings fixed in one position, and that is the best man can hope to do unless he uses a propeller.

Having found out how the wings flap, the next thing is what makes them flap? There are two completely different methods by which insects flap their wings. The most obvious way is the oldest and was developed 350 million years ago by dragonflies. Their wings flap by means of direct muscles. Muscles A pull the wing down.

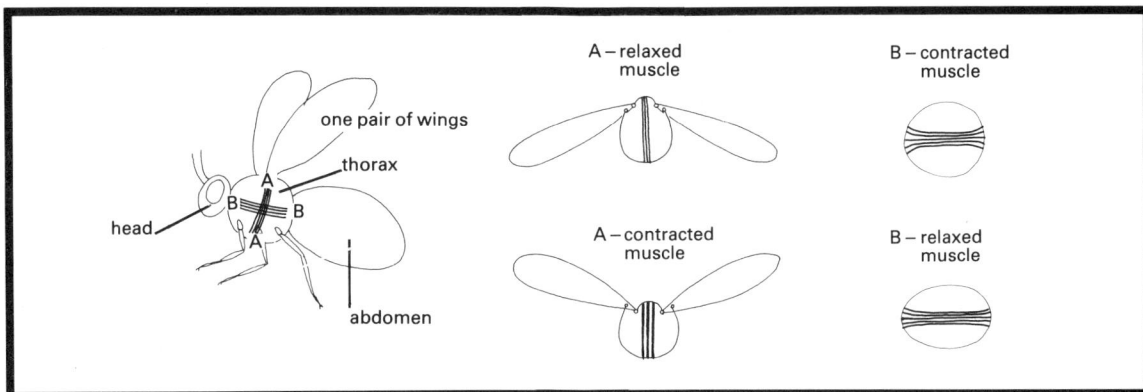

Fly power.

A – relaxed muscle

B – contracted muscle

A – contracted muscle

B – relaxed muscle

one pair of wings

thorax

head

abdomen

Muscles B pull the wing up.

In flies (*Diptera*), the muscles controlling the flap of the wings, and so flight, are not attached to the wings, but alter the shape of the thorax. If the muscles A contract, the thorax is squeezed so that it flattens and the wings are drawn up. To flap down, muscles B squeeze the thorax so that it becomes deeper.

The method has a number of refinements which we need not worry about, except to say that this method, with its extras, is a highly efficient way of flapping the wings. The more efficient flight becomes, the less will be the fuel needed to cover a set distance. This method enables a gnat to flap its wings a thousand times a second.

In a fly, the thorax is packed tight with flight muscles. It is like a 3-litre engine packed under the bonnet of a Mini. Not only that, but the performance of the muscles of a honey bee, for example, in terms of power to weight, is about forty times better than the leg muscles of a human athlete!

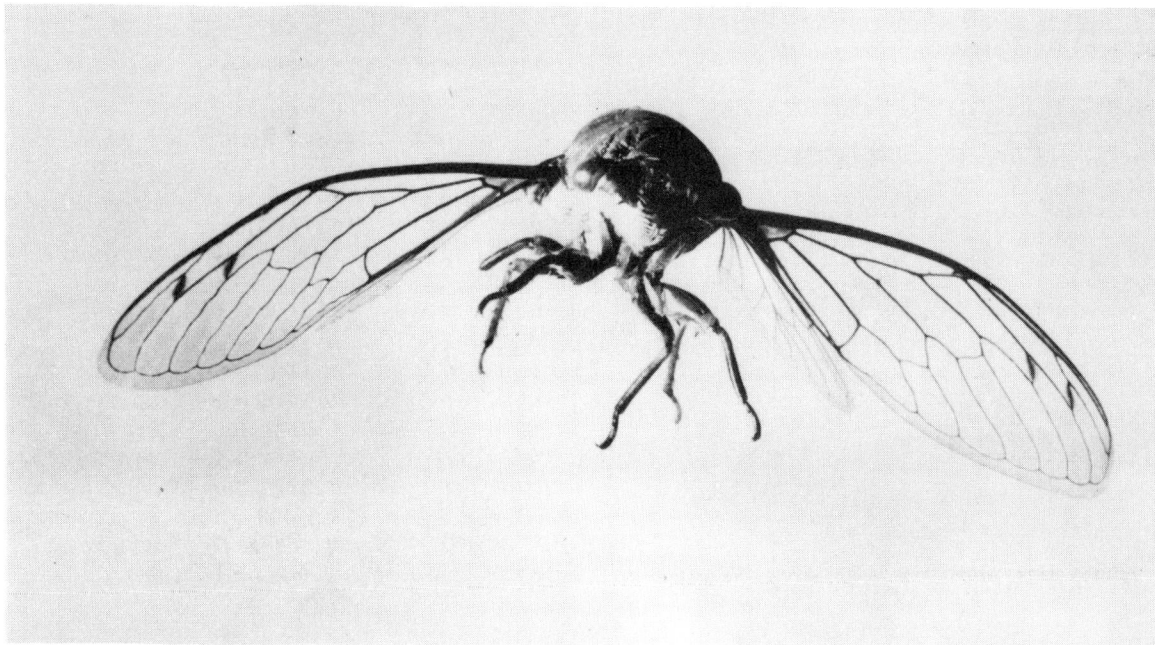

Prehistoric Animals that Flew

How fast can you count? See how many you can count in 10 seconds. Now let's look at some big numbers. If you can count at the rate of two a second, how long would it take you to count a million (1,000,000)? My calculator says – no, you work it out and check your figures with those on page 46. Of course, when you were counting to a million, you'd be working non-stop, day and night, till you'd finished.

Now that we have some idea of how big a number such as 1,000,000 really is, we are going to use even bigger numbers. The Earth is about 4,500 million years old. How long would it take you to count that amount? Look at the Time Scale. Look at the vast time it took for life to evolve to a stage when it could live on land. Then see how evolution has speeded up. See how quickly life took to the air after it had crawled up onto land.

It was the insects who first conquered the air. At the same time as the coal measures were being laid down, amphibians crawled through the forests, and dragonflies flew in the skies.

The ancient dragonflies were very much like the modern spindly speedster.

After the amphibians came the reptiles, a group of successful animals whose rise in the evolutionary ladder was due to the development of the egg. Unlike amphibians, reptiles lay eggs

Life Time Scale (in millions of years).

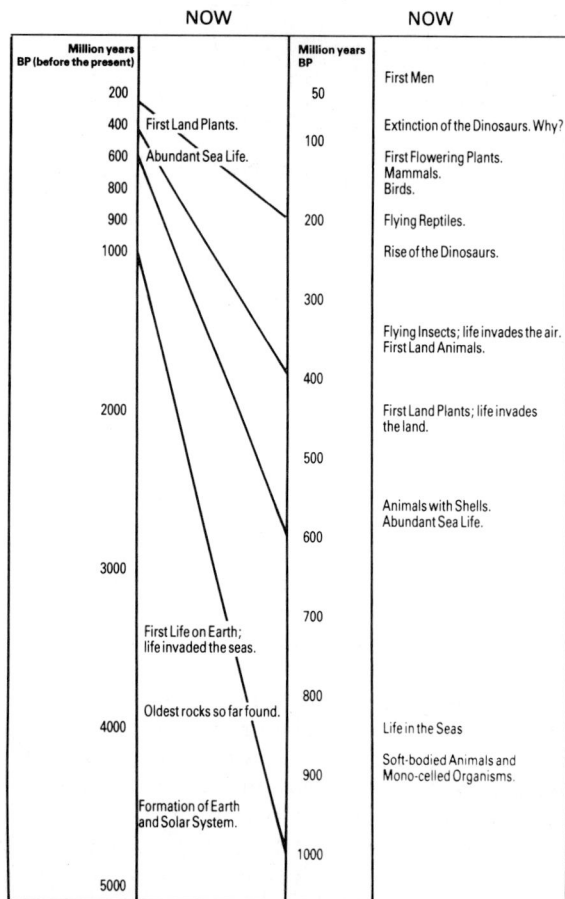

Million years BP (before the present)		NOW	Million years BP	NOW
200			50	First Men
400	First Land Plants.			Extinction of the Dinosaurs. Why?
600	Abundant Sea Life.		100	First Flowering Plants. Mammals.
800				Birds.
900			200	Flying Reptiles.
1000				Rise of the Dinosaurs.
			300	
				Flying Insects; life invades the air. First Land Animals.
			400	
2000				First Land Plants; life invades the land.
			500	
				Animals with Shells. Abundant Sea Life.
			600	
3000				
			700	
	First Life on Earth; life invaded the seas.			
			800	
	Oldest rocks so far found.			
4000				Life in the Seas
			900	Soft-bodied Animals and Mono-celled Organisms.
	Formation of Earth and Solar System.			
			1000	
5000				

that have outer coatings that prevent the loss of water during incubation. Reptiles ruled the roost for 200 million years, and during that time evolved into a huge variety of animals. Some took to the air. The first was a small-sized lizard called Longisquama, who had primitive, scale-covered wings. He lived about 200 million years ago. A number of flying monsters evolved. The Pteranodons (*above*) had a 25-feet wingspan and a weight of around 35 pounds. It seems that they were efficient fliers. In 1975 there was discovered in Texas (where else!) the fossils of a giant among the fliers; a beast that had a 50-feet wingspan. A beast like that makes the stories of Sinbad the Sailor and the giant Roc sound almost plausible.

The stage was set for the next group of dare-devil fliers, the birds. They represent one of the five major groups of animals with backbones, the others being fishes, amphibians, reptiles and mammals. How birds evolved is not known, but the first feathered friend was Archaeopteryx. We talk about something being "as rare as hens' teeth". Well, Archaeopteryx had teeth. He also had claws on his wings. We are not sure that he could fly; he hadn't bones in the right places strong enough to stand the strain of wing flapping. However, there were soon a number of true birds occupying the places left by the extinct flying reptiles, because round about 65 million years ago something happened. We don't know for sure what it was, though there are many theories. The results were dramatic. The lords of creation, masters of sea, land and air, the dinosaurs, died out, and with them disappeared hundreds of different other animals. At one moment in geological history the earth was teeming with life. A short time later, only a handful of animals were left. We don't know what caused the catastrophe, but we do know that nearly all of the big animals had gone for good. Small was beautiful and the small inherited the earth, though they didn't stay small for long. The days of the mammals had arrived and the world was divided. Fishes filled the seas. Mammals took over from the dinosaurs and ruled the land. Birds rode the winds.

Flying Seeds

Have you ever chased a dandelion seed? Have you ever looked at one and seen its delicate structure? Have you ever considered by what methods plants spread their seeds around? Some are most ingenious as, for example, the method used by the plants that fire their seeds from catapults. But many plants use the wind to blow their seeds to pastures new. Here are a few: Sycamore, Ash, Elm, Birch, Hornbeam, Lime, Dandelion, Thistles, Wild Clematis (Traveller's Joy or Old Man's Beard), Gladiolus, Cedar, Bignonia, Pine, Willowherbs, Cotton Grass, Poplar, Willow. All these seeds have something that catches the wind. The Dandelion seed (*page 43*) forms a perfect little parachute, as does the thistle seed.

Some seeds are so small that they do not require a parachute or a sail to ride the winds. The seeds of the orchid are blown out of the capsule in which they form. Fungi are plants that form spores not seeds. The school physics laboratory is likely to have lycopodium powder. It is used in certain sound experiments and is the dried spores of the Giant Puffball. The photograph here shows puffs of spores caused by a drop of water landing on a fungus. Spores are often very small and easily blown about. Even the air over the Canadian Arctic has been shown to contain fungal spores. When spores fall in a suitable place, they grow into a fungus. Quite often the fungus which grows doesn't look much like the spore-producing body. This is because the spore-producing body only grows to produce spores and when it has finished its job it dies. The rest of the fungus is still alive. It all sounds very complicated, but it is a very efficient process and fungi are world-wide in their distribution as their spores hitch a ride on the winds.

How is it possible for a man to parachute to safety from a damaged aeroplane, or for seeds to ride the winds? How is it that a beetle can drop out of a tree and land on the ground unharmed whereas, if you did the same, you would probably break an arm? The Greek, Aristotle (384-322 BC) said that the speed of a falling body depended on its weight: light objects, like feathers, fall slowly; heavy objects, like stones, fall much more quickly. Unfortunately, for the next two thousand years men did not trouble to check his ideas. Then, in the early seventeenth century, Galileo in Italy and Stevin in the Netherlands showed that weights of different sizes fell with equal velocities. Later it was shown that a feather and a lead bullet fell with the same velocity if they were dropped in a vacuum. It is air that slows down a falling feather.

Anything moving through the air has to push the air out of the way. A feather, with its large surface area and small weight, falls slowly. So, if we can increase the area an object offers to the air as it falls, then we can slow down its rate of fall. This is what is done when a man parachutes from an aeroplane. The parachute with its large area of nylon has to push to one side a large amount of air. A tiny seed or spore has a large Area/Weight ratio and the smaller the seed or spore is, the larger the Area/Weight ratio will become.

The simple ideas of areas and weight turn up in all sorts of places: large raindrops falling faster than the drops in mist; babies losing heat much more easily than grown-ups; the settling out of sand and mud in water, and pigments in paint; the activity of finely divided catalysts – ordinary flour burns with difficulty but finely divided flour dust is highly explosive.

To sum up, making grains of a substance smaller by grinding will increase the ratio Area/Weight.

This will increase:
  its chemical reactivity.
  the rate at which it loses heat.
  the ease with which it is blown about by the
    wind.
It will decrease:
  the velocity at which it falls, or settles out
    from a suspension in water.

Clouds, Smoke and Dust

Before we finish we must look at something without which flight, as we know it here on Earth, would be impossible. Air, the invisible stuff all around us, which we take for granted until the winds begin to blow, makes possible the flight of Concorde or of that worrying summer-evening mosquito. It makes this Earth the beautiful place that it is, in spite of all its warts and wrinkles. Yet the most we ever think about air is, "How strong the wind is today" or,

"It's a cold east wind." The poet Shelley recognized the importance of the winds when he wrote:

O wild West Wind, thou breath of Autumn's being,
Thou, from whose unseen presence the leaves dead
Are driven, like ghosts from an enchanter fleeing,
Yellow, and black, and pale, and hectic red,
Pestilence-stricken multitudes;

The wind is a great distributer. It picks up dust and sweet papers, whirls them up in a dancing column, and then dumps them down in a heap. Dust, clouds, leaves and smoke are all swept along. The smoke from your chimney blackens someone else's washing. The fumes from our coal-burning power stations kill the fish in the lakes in Sweden. Volcanic dust blown 10 to 15 miles high into the air is carried right round the world and causes brilliant sunsets. Sand from the Sahara Desert in North Africa falls as Red Dust or Red Rain in Britain. The wind is described as having "scratchy fingers" as it picks up sand grains and hurls them at any obstacle in its path.

Everything that flies is influenced by the wind. Balloons and Airships feel its force and are largely controlled by the direction of its flow. The gales we feel at ground level are mere breezes compared with the 200-mph, 1000-miles-long Jet Streams blowing at a height of 35,000 feet. These are the airman's winds and are used to help airliners.

The winds are produced by the "Weather Machine", a complex natural device which is driven by the heat of the tropics and the cold of the polar regions. All machines need energy to make them work. The energy that drives the "Weather Machine" comes from the Sun.

On most days when we look skywards we see clouds bowling along. They can tell us a lot and studying them can help us to make a weather forecast. There are the cotton wool clouds (cumulus), formed by rising columns of air carrying moisture condensing into tiny droplets of water. Sometimes, on summer days, these cumulus clouds grow into menacing giants stretching seven miles high. These are the thunder clouds. Even the jumbo jets steer clear of them as they have been known to tear aeroplanes to pieces, such is the force of the wind within them.

The whirling pattern of clouds can be seen every evening on the TV weather broadcasts. Weather-men talk about cold and warm fronts, heralding masses of cold and warm air, and tell what to expect next day. Their predictions are based on information about the air pressure, winds and clouds which come into the H.Q. of the Meteorological Office at Bracknell, from weather stations all over the Northern Hemisphere. Balloons carrying instruments and radio transmitters send down to the station information about the weather. This information is fed into a computer at H.Q. to produce weather forecasts for TV, farmers, sailors, airmen and all sorts of people. Even men working in the sewers need rain forecasts to avoid being trapped by the water from a sudden rainstorm.

On an airless world, like the Moon, we would never see kites and balloons, aeroplanes and clouds. The world would be dead, without the squeak of bats and the songs of birds. There would be no need to talk of the weather; there would be none; no summer days with the hum of bees and the sweet scent of honeysuckle; it would be dead, dead, dead.

Glossary

aerodynamics: a study of gases in motion and/or a study of bodies moving through the air.

aeronautics: a study of how to control the flight of aircraft.

biplane: aeroplane with two main wings.

bracing wires: wires used on old aeroplanes to help hold the wings in position.

drag: the force opposing the passage of a body through the air.

gondola: a container slung beneath an airship to carry crew/engine/cargo.

horse power: the British unit of power; it is work done at the rate of 550 foot-pounds per second; 1 HP is equal to 745.7 Watts.

lift: force exerted at perpendicular to the wings due to the motion of air over the wing surfaces (see diagram below).

monoplane: aeroplane with only one main wing.

propellers: large fans driven by engines.

rotors: the revolving wings of autogiros and helicopters.

stress: the force applied to a body when it is pulled or pushed or twisted.

subsonic: below the speed of sound. This varies according to the temperature. At 0°C it is 332 metres per second or approximately 743 miles per hour.

supersonic: above the speed of sound.

thermals: masses of heated rising air.

triplane: an aeroplane with three main wings mounted one above the other.

Answer to question on page 40

"How long would it take you to count to one million?".

5 days, 18 hours, 53 minutes, 20 seconds – non-stop.

Wing lift.

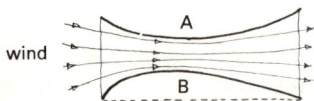

Imagine air is passing through a constriction; it moves faster and there is a drop in pressure. Surfaces A and B tend to be drawn together.

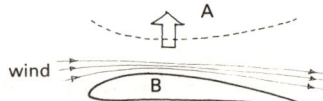

If surface A is removed and surface B is the top surface of a wing, surface B is still drawn in the direction of the arrow.

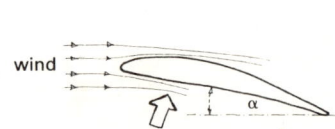

Lift is also provided by the wing flying at an angle α to the wind. Air strikes the underside of the wing and provides an upward force.

Book List

Andrews, Allen, *Back to the Drawing Board: The Evolution of Flying Machines,* David and Charles, 1977

Barnaby, Ralph S., *How to Make and Fly Paper Aircraft,* John Murray, 1971

Barwell, Eve and Bailey, Conrad, *How to Make and Fly Kites,* Studio Vista, 1972

Chant, Christopher, *Aviation, An Illustrated History,* Orbis, 1978

Furniss, Tim, *Man in Space,* Batsford, 1981

Gibbs-Smith, Charles H.,*Aviation,* H.M.S.O., 1970

             Sir George Cayley, H.M.S.O., 1968

             Sir George Cayley's Aeronautics 1796-1855, H.M.S.O., 1962

             The Wright Brothers, H.M.S.O., 1963

             A History of Flying, Batsford, 1953

Green W., Swanborough Gordon, *Illustrated Anatomy of the World's Fighter,* Salamander Books

Hargreaves B., Chinnery, M., *Butterflies and Moths,* Collins, 1981

Heinzel, H., Fitter, R., Parslow, J., *Birds of Britain and Europe,* Collins, 1974

Jackson, Donald, Dale, *The Aeronauts,* Time-Life, 1981

Man, J., *The Day of the Dinosaur,* Bison Books, 1978

McNeil, Mary Jean, *The Know How Book of Flying Models,* Usborne Publishing Ltd., 1975

Mondey, David, *Civil Aircraft,* Hamlyn Publishing, 1981

Munson, K., *Pioneer Aircraft 1903-1914,* Blandford Press, 1969

Nachtigall, Werner, *Insects in Flight,* Allen and Unwin, 1974

Pelham, David, *Kites,* Penguin, 1976

Stever, H. Guyford and Haggerty, James J., *Flight,* Time-Life, 1971

Sully, Nina, *Looking at Insects,* Batsford, 1982

Taylor, J.W.R., *Aircraft of World War I,* Hippo Books No.16., Longacre Press

Welch, A. and L., *The Story of Gliding,* John Murray, 1965

Wragg, David, *Flight with Power: The First Ten Years,* Barrie and Jenkins, 1978

Yalden, B.W., and Morris, P.A., *The Lives of Bats,* David and Charles, 1975

Model Aeroplanes

Useful monthly magazines for would-be model aeroplane builders are *Aeromodeller, Radio Modeller, Radio Control Models and Electronics.* The Ripmax Modellers' Handbook is published by Ripmax Models Ltd, Ripmax Corner, Green Street, Enfield, Middlesex EN3 7SJ.

If you want to start aeromodelling, go to someone who builds models and ask for advice. Please do not start on a complicated scale model to start off. Good Luck.

Index